CANDLE MAKING

FOR FUN!

by Dana Meachen Rau

Content Adviser: Jim Pitittieri, Former Vice President of Manufacturing, Yankee Candle Company, Conway, Massachusetts
Reading Adviser: Frances J. Bonacci, Ed.D, Reading Specialist, Cambridge, Massachusetts

Compass Point Books Minneapolis, Minnesota

Compass Point Books
3109 West 50th Street, #115
Minneapolis, MN 55410

Visit Compass Point Books on the Internet at www.compasspointbooks.com
or e-mail your request to custserv@compasspointbooks.com

Photographs©: Capstone Press/TJ Thoraldson Digital Photography, front cover (top left); Steve Gorton, front cover (bottom left), 33; Dmitry Ternovoy/Shutterstock, front cover (top right); Elena Kalistratova/Shutterstock, front cover (bottom right); Jakub Niezabitowski/iStockphoto, 5 (left); Edyta Linek/iStockphoto, 5 (right); Joshua Haviv/iStockphoto, 6; Nicolette Neish/iStockphoto, 7; Julián Rovagnati/BigStockPhoto, 8; Cristian Lazzari/iStockphoto, 9; Deborah Albers/iStockphoto, 10–11; Anness Publishing, 13, 17, 20, 21, 22, 23, 24–25, 27 (bottom), 29 (left), 30; Craig Veltri/iStockphoto, 13 (bottom), 14 (bottom); Denise Torres/iStockphoto, 14–15, 19 (top); Matthew Scherf/iStockphoto, 15 (right), 18–19; Laura Stone/iStockphoto, 27 (top); Martin Cerny/iStockphoto, 29 (right); Carl Subick/BigStockPhoto, 31; Enna van Duinen/BigStockPhoto, 32; Lorenzo Pastore/iStockphoto, 34; José Luis Gutiérrez/iStockphoto, 35 (all); Ethan Myerson/iStockphoto, 36; Photodisc, 37; Chris Schmidt/iStockphoto, 38–39; Mike Manzano/iStockphoto, 40–41, 41 (right); Shawn Kretz/iStockphoto, 42 (top); Brian McEntire/iStockphoto, 42 (bottom); Willie B. Thomas/iStockphoto, 43 (all); Brian McEntire/iStockphoto, 44 (left); Terry J Alcorn/iStockphoto, 44 (right); Lise Gagne/iStockphoto, 45 (left); Gunther Beck/iStockphoto, 45 (right); iStockphoto, 47.

Editors: Lionel Bender and Brenda Haugen
Designer: Bill SMITH STUDIO
Page Production: Ben White and Ashlee Schultz
Photo Researcher: Suzanne O'Farrell
Art Director: Jaime Martens
Creative Director: Keith Griffin
Editorial Director: Nick Healy
Managing Editor: Catherine Neitge
Candle Making for Fun! was produced for Compass Point Books by Bender Richardson White, UK

Library of Congress Cataloging-in-Publication Data
Rau, Dana Meachen, 1971–
  Candle making for fun! / by Dana Meachen Rau.
    p. cm. — (For fun)
  ISBN-13: 978-0-7565-3276-5 (library binding)
  ISBN-10: 0-7565-3276-0 (library binding)
1. Candlemaking. I. Title. II. Series.
  TT896.5.R385 2008
  745.593'32—dc22   2007004894

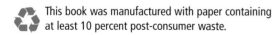
This book was manufactured with paper containing
at least 10 percent post-consumer waste.

Table of Contents

Note: In this book, there are two kinds of vocabulary words. Candle Making Words to Know are words specific to candle making. They are defined on page 46. Other Words to Know are helpful words that are not related only to candle making. They are defined on page 47.

Lovely Light

When the power goes out, the lights don't work. You might light a candle to see. Before electricity, candles were among the few sources of light people had when the sun went down.

Today people still use candles. They might light them to celebrate a holiday in church or at their temple. A candle can also be a special gift for someone you care about or used for a special event such as a birthday.

Candles are even more special when you make them yourself. For thousands of years, people have been making candles. Long ago, it was a messy, smelly job. Today you can find all you need at a craft store or even at home. And the process is a lot more fun!

Fire Safety

Candles can be beautiful, but they can be dangerous, too. You need to be safe when burning and making candles. You should never make or use candles without an adult around. See pages 18 and 19 for safety rules about candles.

People use candles for celebrations and to decorate a table for dinner. They light them to fill the room with a pleasant smell. Candles come in many shapes and colors.

From Torches to Light Bulbs

The Statue of Liberty holds a torch high over New York.

Candles have been used for centuries. The candles used by ancient Egyptians and Romans were torches made from reeds dipped in tallow. Tallow is a waxy substance made from melted fat from cattle or sheep.

In the Middle Ages, people made candles from beeswax. Colonial Americans in the 1600s and 1700s used bayberries that made a wax with a nice color and odor. During the boom of the whaling industry in the late 1700s, people found that oil from the sperm whale could also be made into a candle wax.

In the mid 1800s, paraffin greatly changed candle making. Paraffin was a substance left over from the processing of oil for petroleum. It was not too expensive and gave off no smell.

Of course, when the light bulb was invented in 1879, people didn't rely as much on candles. People started using candles more for decoration and to create a mood and emotion rather than for their light.

All Shapes and Colors

What type of candles do you use? Candles can be made in any shape and any color. Some basic types of candles are:

Tapers: Tapers are long and slim. Tapers stand best in tall, slender candleholders.

Pillars: Pillar candles stand on their own and are usually 3 inches (7.6 centimeters) wide or more. They can be round, square, or other shapes. Often pillar candles of different heights are grouped together.

Votives: Votives are small, round candles made in molds. They come in many scents and colors. They fit into small glass cup candleholders.

Floating candles: Floating candles are made by molding or cutting small shapes from wax. They are often shaped like flowers or little tarts. Since wax floats, these candles can be grouped together in a wide bowl of water.

Tea lights: Tea lights are very small candles that sit in their own metal dishes. They are sometimes used to heat scented wax in special pots.

Flares: A flare has a candle on the end of a long wooden stick. Flares can be stuck into the ground outside to give light in the evening.

Fuel and Flames

A candle is a very simple system. The wax and the wick are all the candle needs to make light.

The wax is the fuel for the candle. When you light the wick, the heat of the flame melts the wax around it. The wick absorbs this liquid wax and sucks it up to the top. The heat of the flame changes this liquid into a gas called wax vapor. The wick brings the wax up to become vapor. It is the vapor that burns. The wick curls and turns to ash.

The flame also needs oxygen to keep burning. When you use a candle snuffer, you can see this in action. A snuffer extinguishes, or puts out, the flame by cutting off its supply of oxygen from the air.

A candle drips when there is too much melted wax. The wick can't absorb, or take up, the wax fast enough, so it may spill over the sides of the candle. This sometimes happens when the size of the wick is too small compared to the size of the candle. If a wick is too small, the extra wax around it can also drown out the flame. If a wick is too big, it can create a lot of smoke and a large flame.

Tricky Wicks

How can a trick candle relight after you blow it out? The trick candle wick has magnesium, a type of metal, added in. When you blow out the flame, there is still a burning bit on the wick. This is hot enough to relight the magnesium. Then the magnesium relights the wax vapors.

Wax and Wicks

Most candles are made from paraffin. This often comes in large slabs, 1-pound (0.45-kilogram) blocks, small chunks, or pellets. You can buy it already colored or add your own dye.

Depending on the type of candle you are making, you might have to mix your paraffin with a substance called stearin. It comes from palm nuts but used to come from tallow. Stearin makes paraffin contract, or get smaller, when it cools. So stearin makes it easier for you to get a candle out of a mold. Stearin also helps the candle harden and burn longer. In some stores, you may be able to buy paraffin with the right amount of stearin already mixed in.

Wicks

Some wicks are made of paper, and some are made of cotton. Braided cotton wicks, made up of lots of small strings twisted together, are the type most candle makers use. The package will often tell you the size of the wick to buy for the size of the candle you plan to make. You can buy wicks in small packages or in large spools. A store might also sell specific types of wicks for each type of candle.

Appliqué wax is used to decorate candles. You put it on the outside of a cooled candle. It comes in sheets to cut into shapes.

Beeswax is made from the wax bees create in their hives. It comes in blocks, chunks, or in flat sheets.

Bayberry wax is made from small, grayish bayberries. People don't add color or scent to bayberry wax. It smells nice and is a pale green color.

13

Hold Everything!

Candles come in all sorts of shapes—tall, short, round, square. You can even make candles shaped like animals or fake food! Candle makers use molds to hold the wax and give each candle its unique shape.

You can buy molds made from glass, plastic, or metal at a craft store. These types of molds can be used over and over again. Molds for more detailed shapes are made from latex, a type of rubber. Your kitchen might be filled with molds you can use, too. A milk or orange juice carton makes a great square mold. You can use candy molds to make floating candles. You can even create your own mold out of sturdy cardboard or plastic and strong tape.

Container Candles

Container candles are made in a similar way to molded candles, but you never take them out of their containers. They are like candles and candleholders all in one! If you want to see the candle inside, use a glass container. If you just want to see the top, use a ceramic bowl or even a clean clay flowerpot. Just be sure the container can sit still on a flat surface without tipping over.

Candle Maker's Tools

Double boiler: A double boiler is a pot with two levels. In the bottom pot, you boil water, and in the top pot, you melt the wax. The wax pot should never go directly on the stove.

Mold seal: Mold seal covers the hole in the bottom of a mold to keep the wax in and water out.

Wick tabs or clips: These small metal objects hold the bottoms of wicks in place in the candles.

Dye: Some color dye comes as a dye disc or slab. Some dyes come in powder form.

Scents: Candle scents come in small jars or in small slabs of wax.

Dipping can: When making dipped candles, you will need a tall metal can to hold the hot wax.

Skewers: These will hold the wicks in place when you make molded or container candles.

Thermometer:
Thermometers show you how hot your wax is getting. You need to use a special wax thermometer or candy thermometer designed to take high temperatures. Do not use a thermometer that checks body temperature.

Pouring pitcher and molds:
A pouring pitcher can be used as the top pot in a double boiler to melt the wax and pour it into a mold.

Keep It Safe

The most important thing to remember when making and burning candles is to KEEP IT SAFE! Melted wax and open flames can cause a lot of damage to anything that burns—clothing, your house, and most especially you! You should always have an adult with you when you work with candles.

Hot Molten Wax

Never leave the pot of melting wax alone. Heat the wax slowly. You don't want it to reach a temperature above 180 degrees Fahrenheit (82 degrees Celsius) for most projects. An electric stove is safer than gas, because there is no open flame. If the wax catches on fire, turn off the heat. Smother the flame with a pot lid or baking soda. Also, have a fire extinguisher within reach in case it is a bigger fire. Never try to put out a wax fire with water. Wear oven mitts and an apron to protect you from hot wax.

Snuffing Candles

When you extinguish the candle, it is best to use a candle snuffer. This is a tool made of metal with a long handle and a cup on the end that covers the flame to extinguish it. Once the flame is out, wait for the wax to turn solid before you move the candle.

Before you light a candle, trim the wick to $1/4$ inch (0.65 cm). The top of the candle should be free of old matches or pieces of wick. Never leave a burning candle unattended. Your candle should always be in a candleholder and on a flat surface where it cannot fall or be knocked over. Do not put the candle near papers or other materials that could catch on fire or near an air draft that could blow on the flame.

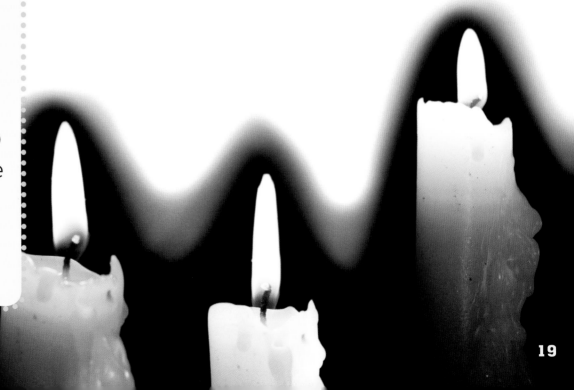

Solid to Liquid

1. Let's get started! Fill the lower pot of your double boiler with a few inches of water, and heat until it boils. Lower the heat so the water is simmering. If too much water evaporates, add more. Never let the bottom pot get dry.

2. Put on the top pot, or a pouring pitcher, and add the wax. Stir the mix. Check the temperature often.

3. You need to prepare your wick by letting it soak up wax so that it burns more easily. This is called priming the wick. Drop a length of wick into the wax, and immediately remove it. When the wax cools, straighten the wick, and put it aside.

4. If you are going to use stearin (for a candle that will need to come out

Materials

- Double boiler
- Wax and stearin
- Wooden spoon
- Wax thermometer
- Wick

of a mold), heat it in another double boiler. In general, you need one part stearin to every 10 parts wax.

5. Once the wax and stearin are melted, you can add color and scent. (See pages 28-29). Pour any extra wax into a container so that it will cool into a slab that you can use again.

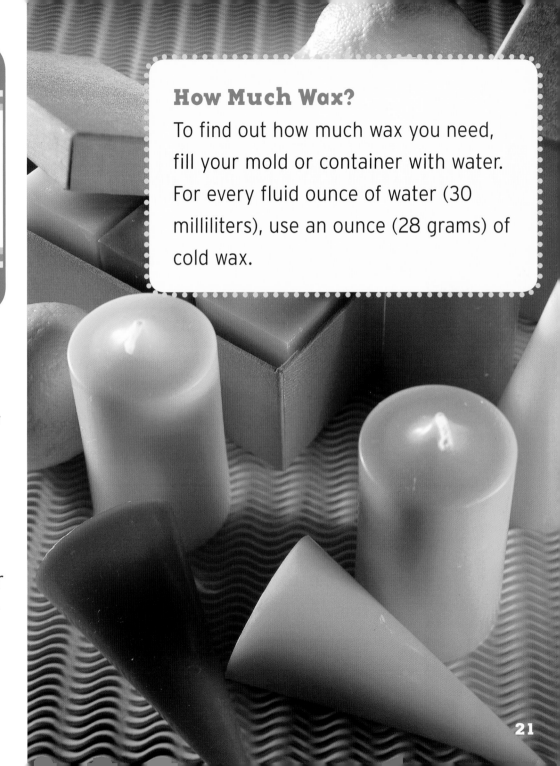

How Much Wax?

To find out how much wax you need, fill your mold or container with water. For every fluid ounce of water (30 milliliters), use an ounce (28 grams) of cold wax.

Molded Candle

For this project you can use a household drink carton or a special candle mold.

1. Clean your carton, cut off the top, and poke a small hole in the bottom.

2. Use a length of wick 3 inches (7.5 cm) longer than your candle. Prime the wick. (See pages 20-21). Tie one end of the wick around the skewer, and lay the skewer across the open top of the carton. Thread the other end of the wick through the hole, pull it until straight, and secure the wick with the mold seal. Make sure the wick is central.

3. Pour the hot wax into the open top of the carton, and then tap the sides to get rid of air bubbles.

4. Place the carton into a deep bowl or bucket. Put a weight (such as a plate) on the top of the carton, and be sure the carton is sitting level.

5. Fill the bowl with cold water up to the level of the wax. As the wax hardens, pull the wick back to a central position.

6. After the wax cools for an hour, a well will have formed around the wick. Prick the surface of the well, and "top up" the well with reheated wax.

7. Let the wax cool again. Then remove the carton from the water, take off the mold seal, and gently pull your candle out of the carton. Cut the wick off at the bottom. At the top, cut the wick to about 1/4 inch (0.65 cm).

Materials

- Small juice or milk carton
- Scissors
- Wick
- Wooden skewers
- Mold seal
- Melted wax and stearin
- Bowl and cold water

Plant Pot Candle

A container candle is made in a similar way to a molded candle. Here, a clay plant pot is used as a container, but you can use any heatproof item. Use colored or scented wax as desired (see pages 28-29).

1. Prepare a primed wick 3 inches (7.5 cm) longer than your candle. Attach it to a wick tab or clip. (See pages 16-17, 20-21).

2. Glue the wick tab firmly to the bottom center of the plant pot. Let the glue dry. Tie the other end of the wick to the skewer laid across the top of the plant pot. Be sure the wick is straight and centered in the pot.

Materials

- Plant pot
- Wick and wick tab or clip
- Wax glue
- Wooden skewers
- Melted wax
- Bowl and cold water
- Scissors

3. Pour in melted wax close to the top of the plant pot. Tap the sides gently to get rid of air bubbles. Place the plant pot in a small bowl. Put a weight on top of the pot, and fill the bowl with cold water to the level of the wax but no more. Recenter the wick.

4. Let it sit for about an hour. Prick the well around the wick with a skewer. Top up the wax by pouring more heated wax into the well to just below the level before.

5. Let the wax dry completely. Cut the wick to about $1/4$ inch (0.65 cm).

6. Place your finished plant pot candle on a clay saucer—the perfect candleholder!

Dipped Tapers

Dipped tapers are made by dipping the wick into a tall container of wax. They are made in pairs joined by the wick.

1. Before you melt the wax, set up a place to dry your candles. Place a piece of wooden board at the edge of a table so that your tapers can hang off of each side. On the floor under this, lay newspapers to catch dripping wax.

2. Heat the wax to about 160 degrees F (71 degrees C), and keep it at this temperature. Take your long piece of wick, and fold it in half. Hold the wick in the center, and dip the halves into the wax for three seconds. Lift out the wicks, hang them over the board, and let them cool for one to three minutes.

3. Continue dipping for three seconds, cooling for three minutes, until the candles are as

Wax Tips

The higher your dipping can, the longer your tapers can be. But you will need more wax. A can that is 12 inches (30.5 cm) high needs about 6 1/4 pounds (3 kg) of wax. Keeping the wax at 160 degrees F (71 degrees C) (a little cooler than usual) keeps the wax from melting the previous layer each time you dip.

thick as you want them. This may take up to 30 dips. Be very careful to hold the wick so that the candles do not touch, or they could stick to each other.

4. Let your candles cool completely hanging over the board. You can cut the wick to separate your candles.

Colors and Scents

If you are making a lilac-scented candle, your candle could be light purple. Or if you are making a cookie-scented candle, the color could be light brown. Here's how to make a multicolor, single-scent candle.

1. Melt the wax and stearin to 180 degrees F (82 degrees C). (See pages 20-21). Divide up the melted stearin into as many pots as you want colors. Add a different color and some scent to each pot. For each color, shave off tiny bits of the dye disc, or put in just a little bit of the powder. For the scent, put a few drops of the perfume into each pot. Stir in the colors and scent.

2. Add melted wax to each pot of melted stearin mix. In general, you need 10 parts wax to one part stearin. Stir the melted wax and stearin together thoroughly.

3. Prepare your wick, and position it in the center of the mold. (See pages 20-21, 22-23).

4. Pour in the contents of one pot, and wait about 45 minutes until the wax mix is hard on the edges but rubbery when you poke it in the center. Then pour in the next color mix, and wait for that layer to cool. Repeat for as many stripes as you wish. Remove your candle from the mold, and trim the wick.

Finishing Touches

As well as adding colors, you can decorate the outside of your candle. Appliqué wax can be cut into shapes and glued onto the surface. Or glue on dried petals with wax glue.

Materials

- 2 or more double boilers
- Wax and stearin
- Colors
- Scent
- Wick
- Candle mold and mold seal

Rolled Candles

Beeswax usually comes in sheets that do not have to be melted to make candles. The sheets are usually colored and scented.

1. For each candle, use an 8 inch x 16 inch (20 cm x 41 cm) sheet of beeswax cut in half. Lay the sheet on a flat surface with one of the shorter ends of the rectangle facing you.

2. Carefully lay the wick out straight along the end, with some hanging off on either side.

3. Start rolling the beeswax over the wick just enough to completely cover it. With the warmth from your fingers, gently pinch the wax around the wick to make sure it does not slip out.

4. Keep rolling away from you. Roll the sheet tightly and evenly until you are about 1 inch (2.5 cm) from the far end.

5. Heat this last edge with a hair dryer to make the beeswax extra sticky and soft. Don't do it too long, or the wax will start melting. Roll the candle to the end, and press this edge very gently to be sure it is sealed.

6. Trim the wick at the bottom of the candle so that it is flush with the end. At the top, trim the wick to $1/4$ inch (0.65 cm).

Materials

• Sheet of beeswax
• Wick
• Hair dryer
• Scissors

Lanterns

Candleholders can be made of wood, tin, glass, brass, or pewter. People put candles in lanterns, in bottles, and on candelabras. A nice rock, flower pot, hollowed out gourd, or piece of fruit can hold a candle, too.

Materials

- Glass jar
- Glass paint or paint pens
- Glue
- Beads
- Sand
- A votive candle

This "lantern" is made by carving a face into a pumpkin and placing a candle inside.

1. Take a clean, dry, wide-mouthed glass jar, and decorate the outside with paint. You can make stripes, swirls, or write someone's name if you are giving it as a gift.

2. Glue on more details, such as beads or mosaic tiles.

3. Fill the jar about halfway with sand.

4. Place a votive candle into the sand so that it is level and secure.

5. Ask an adult to help you light the candle.

You can buy ready made lantern cases in craft shops and hardware stores.

Lighting the World

Besides seeing candles as decorations in your home, think about other places you might see them. Candles are often found in churches and temples of many religions. In Christian churches all around the world, candles stand on the altar and are lit for services. Some churches have small chapels on the side where you can go to light a candle to represent a special prayer you might have.

Candles are also lit to remember those who have died. Perhaps you have lit a candle for this reason? In Mexico, and other Central and South American countries, some people celebrate the Day of the Dead on November 2. It is a happy time when families remember those relatives who have died and decorate altars in their homes with food, flowers, and candles.

Buddhists in Thailand, and in many other countries, might have a home shrine. Here they take a moment each day to meditate. A Buddhist shrine might have a statue of Buddha, fresh flowers, and candles.

Candles also bring people together for common causes. To remember those who have died from cancer or other diseases, or when people want to come together for hope or peace, they might hold a candlelight vigil. They gather outside, each person with a small lit taper, to join together for a cause.

There have even been some worldwide candle lightings, organized so that people all over the globe light candles at a certain time to unite for a common idea.

Celebrating Special Days

Happy birthday! Time to blow out your candles and make a wish! A birthday cake is often dotted with the same number of candles as a celebrant's age. Candles for birthday cakes even come in number shapes.

The religious observations of Christmas, the Sabbath, and Diwali would not be the same without candles. Many people light the candles of an Advent wreath during the four weeks leading up to Christmas. Jewish people celebrate the start of the Sabbath by lighting two candles. They light eight candles to celebrate Hanukkah. Hindu people light many candles on the festival of Diwali.

Candlemas

Candlemas is a holiday with ancient roots that began as a way to bring light to a long, dark winter. It is celebrated on February 2. People thought that the weather on that day would decide the weather for the rest of winter. This holiday has a new tradition today—as groundhogs "predict" how long the rest of winter will be.

Patron Saint of Light

In Sweden, people celebrate St. Lucia day. St. Lucia is the patron saint of light. Girls wear traditional white dresses with red sashes. On their heads, they wear crowns of candles.

Candle Factories

Candle making started as a humble profession, as people made candles by melting wax over their own open fires. In the 1200s, the first candle-making guilds formed in Paris, and they performed an important service. Whether people made candles themselves or relied on the craftsmanship of others, candles were needed by every household.

In 1834, a man named Joseph Morgan invented a machine that could make candles quicker. It continuously pushed molded candles out of a cylinder shape. Other machines with large racks could dip many tapers at a time. Today machines in factories make candles in a variety of ways. People still make candles at home, but candle making has also become a huge industry.

In the United States, there are more than 400 candle manufacturers. It is estimated that they sell about $2 billion of candles every year.

The Oldest Candle Makers

Rathbornes Candles, in Dublin, Ireland, was founded in 1488. It is still in business today. Some workers make candles with modern machines, while their master chandlers still use traditional methods to make others.

Candles can be bought in many places. Gift shops and home stores have shelves filled with candles in many styles. You can pick up candles in the grocery store or drug store. Some candles cost less than a dollar. Others can cost hundreds of dollars. Most people buy candles for the smell they give.

The Yankee Candle Company

Mike Kittredge made his own candles when he was young. Just before Christmas in 1969 when he was 16 years old, Kittredge did not have enough money to buy his mother a present. So he gathered up his old crayons, melted them on the stove, and poured them into a milk carton. The result was his first candle.

A neighbor bought the candle from him. Kittredge bought paraffin with the money and made two more. One he gave to his mother. The other he sold. That is how Kittredge founded The Yankee Candle Company. The company has grown into the leading maker of scented candles in the United States.

The most famous Yankee Candle store is the main headquarters based in South Deerfield, Massachusetts. It is one of the most popular tourist stops in New England, with 2.5 million people coming to visit each year. Some have even called it the "Disneyland of candles."

The Votive Room

One of the most fun rooms in Yankee Candle in South Deerfield, Massachusetts, is the room of scented votives. It is filled with bins of candles in every smell you can imagine.

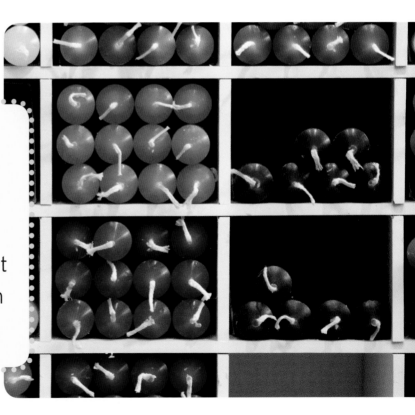

What Happened When?

100 B.C. — 1100 A.D. — 1300 — 1400 — 1500 — 1600 — 1700

100 B.C. Ancient Romans made clay lamps, filled them with olive oil, and used wicks made from plant fibers.

1200s Candle-making guilds form in Paris.

1488 Rathborne's Candles founded in Dublin, Ireland. The company is still in business today.

Late 1600s Colonists find that abundant bayberries in America make a clean, nice smelling wax to use in candles.

1700s Whaling leads to the use of spermaceti in candles. Spermaceti was derived from the oil in the head of the sperm whale.

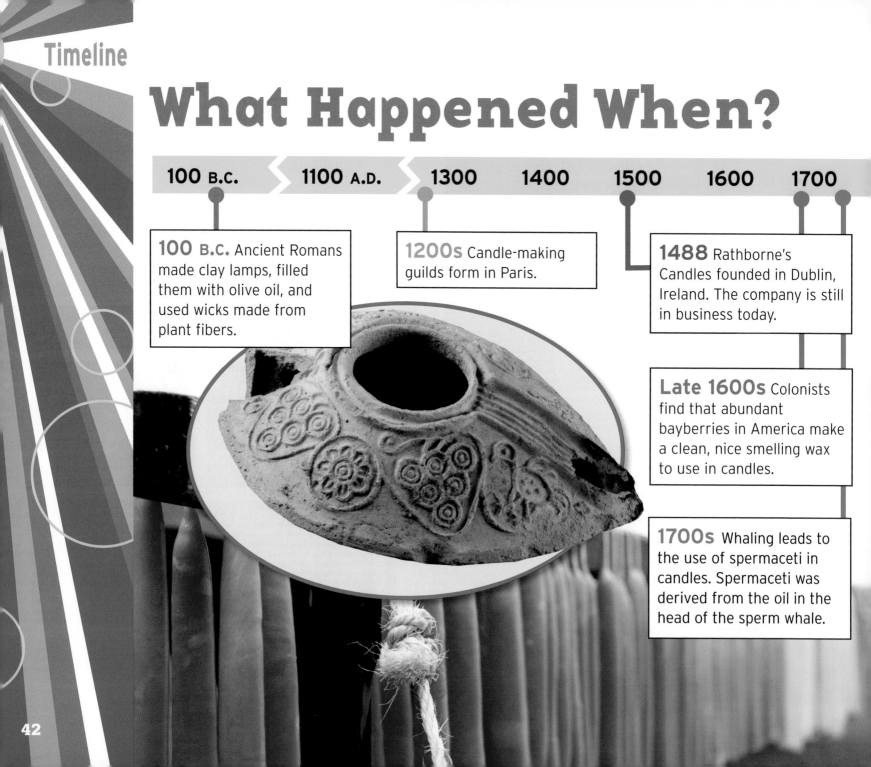

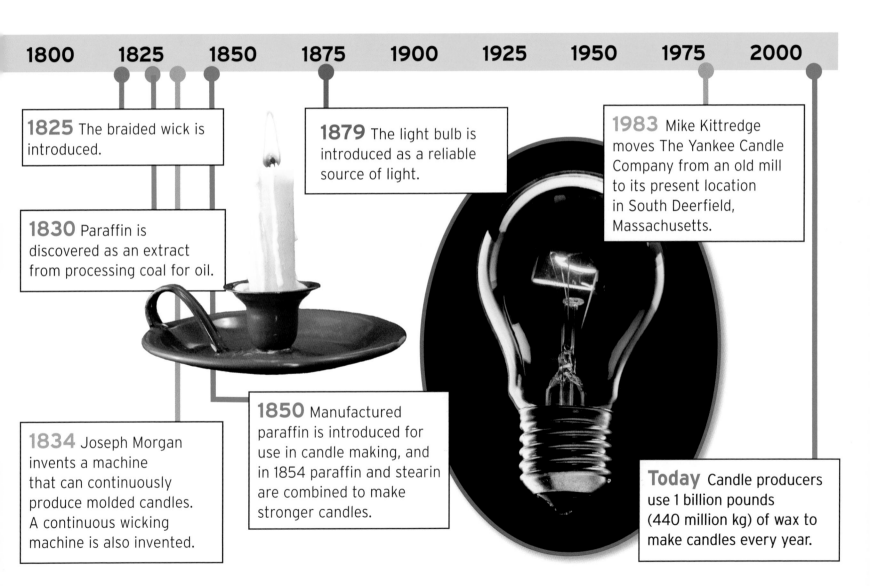

| 1800 | 1825 | 1850 | 1875 | 1900 | 1925 | 1950 | 1975 | 2000 |

1825 The braided wick is introduced.

1830 Paraffin is discovered as an extract from processing coal for oil.

1834 Joseph Morgan invents a machine that can continuously produce molded candles. A continuous wicking machine is also invented.

1850 Manufactured paraffin is introduced for use in candle making, and in 1854 paraffin and stearin are combined to make stronger candles.

1879 The light bulb is introduced as a reliable source of light.

1983 Mike Kittredge moves The Yankee Candle Company from an old mill to its present location in South Deerfield, Massachusetts.

Today Candle producers use 1 billion pounds (440 million kg) of wax to make candles every year.

43

Fun Candle Facts

In colonial America, making candles was often the chore of women and girls. They made the candles by hand at home. It took up to 15 pounds (6.8 kg) of bayberries to make 1 pound (0.45 kg) of wax. So many people still used tallow from animals.

Last names often come from people's occupations. A chandler was a person who made and sold candles. So someone with the last name Chandler might be related to a candle maker from long ago.

44

U.S. candle manufacturers make about 1,000 to 2,000 types of candles. And there are about 10,000 scents to choose from.

In the ninth century, candles helped people keep time. Hours were marked at regular intervals on the side of a timekeeping candle. The candle burned for 24 hours. You could tell how much time had passed by how short the candle had become.

Candle Making Words to Know

appliqué wax: wax that comes in thin sheets to decorate the outside of candles

bayberries: fruits that can be boiled to make wax

beeswax: wax created by bees in their hives

chandler: someone who makes and sells candles

dipping can: tall metal container used for making tapers

double boiler: two pots, one inside another, used for melting wax

dye: colors you can add to a candle

flammable: able to catch on fire

flare: candle on the end of a long, wooden stick that goes into the ground

flashpoint: temperature at which the vapors from wax can catch on fire

floating candles: small candles that float in water

latex: type of rubber or plastic used to make molds

molds: tools used to give candles their shapes

paraffin: commonly used candle wax derived from processing oil

pillar: candle that stands on its own, that can be round or square

primed wick: wick that has already absorbed some wax

scent: smell you can add to a candle

snuffer: metal tool used to put out a candle flame

stearin: substance that makes paraffin contract

tallow: waxy substance made from melted fat from cattle or sheep

tapers: long, slim candles made in pairs by dipping

thermometer: device that lets you know how hot or cool something is

topping up: making the top of the candle smooth by pouring more wax into the well around the wick

votives: small candles made in molds

wick: cotton or paper string in the middle of the candle that absorbs the wax

wick tabs or clips: small metal devices used to hold wicks in place

Other Words to Know

absorb: suck up, like a sponge

Advent wreath: round evergreen wreath with four candles lit during the month before Christmas

altar: table often set up in the front of a church or temple

candelabra: a branched candlestick or lamp with many candles or lightbulbs

ember: a bit of burning material left over from a fire

guilds: groups of people who perform similar tasks or have common skills

oxygen: one of the parts of air that flames need to burn

shrine: place set aside to pray or meditate

temple: place of worship

vapor: gaseous state of a substance

vigil: time when people keep watch or pray together

Where To Learn More

AT THE LIBRARY

Brooks, Dana Marie. *Cut and Carve Candles: Beautiful Candles to Dip, Carve, Twist, and Curl.* Ashville, N.C.: Lark Books, 2004.

Owen, Cheryl. *Candle Making.* Chanhassen, Minn.: Creative Publishing International, 2002.

Spear, Sue. *Candle Making in a Weekend: Inspirational Ideas and Practical Projects.* Cincinnati, Ohio: North Light Books, 1999.

ON THE ROAD

The Yankee Candle Company
25 Greenfield Road
South Deerfield, MA 01373
413/665-2929

ON THE WEB

For more information on this topic, use FactHound.

1. Go to www.facthound.com
2. Type in this book ID: 0756532760
3. Click on the *Fetch It* button.

FactHound will find the best Web sites for you.

INDEX

ABOUT THE AUTHOR

Dana Meachen Rau has written more than 200 books for children, both fiction and nonfiction. Always busy with her hands, she loves to write, knit, sew, draw, and make almost anything she can imagine. She lives in Burlington, Connecticut, with her husband and children.